Contents

NEBS MANAGEMENT DEVELOPMENT

SUPER SERIES

THIRD EDITION
Managing People

Securing the
Right People

Published for
&NEBS Management   *by*

Pergamon
Flexible
Learning

Pergamon Flexible Learning
An imprint of Butterworth-Heinemann
Linacre House, Jordan Hill, Oxford OX2 8DP
225 Wildwood Avenue, Woburn, MA 01801-2041
A division of Reed Educational and Professional Publishing Ltd

℞ A member of the Reed Elsevier plc group

OXFORD AUCKLAND BOSTON
JOHANNESBURG MELBOURNE NEW DELHI

First published 1986
Second edition 1991
Third edition 1997
Reprinted 1998, 1999, 2000

© NEBS Management 1986, 1991, 1997

British Library Cataloguing in Publication Data
A catalogue record for this book is available from the British Library

ISBN 0 7506 3315 8

Whilst every effort has been made to contact copyright
holders, the author would like to hear from anyone
whose copyright has unwittingly been infringed.

The views expressed in this work are those
of the authors and do not necessarily reflect
those of the National Examining Board for
Supervision and Management or of the publisher.

NEBS Management Project Manager: Diana Thomas
Author: Pip Hardy
Editor: Ian Bloor
Series Editor: Diana Thomas
Based on previous material by: Joe Johnson
Composition by Genesis Typesetting, Rochester, Kent
Printed and bound in Great Britain

Workbook introduction

Here are the workbook titles in each module which link with *Securing the Right People*, should you wish to extend your study to other Super Series workbooks. There is a brief description of each workbook in the *User Guide*.

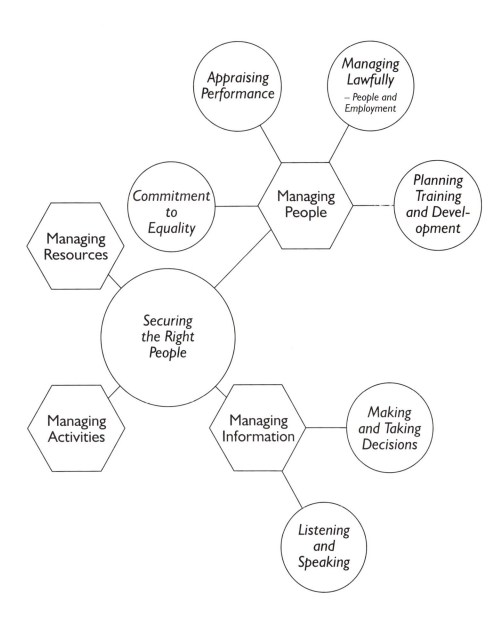

2 S/NVQ links

This workbook relates to the following elements:

C7.1   Contribute to identifying personnel requirements
C7.2   Contribute to selecting required personnel

It is designed to help you demonstrate the following Personal Competences:

- thinking and taking decisions;
- building teams.

3 Workbook objectives

In the following pages I offer nothing more than simple facts, plain arguments and common sense; and have no other preliminaries to settle with the reader, other than that he will divest himself of prejudice and prepossession, and suffer his reason and his feelings to determine for themselves; that he will put on, or rather than he will not put off, the true character of a man, and generously enlarge his views beyond the present day.

Thomas Paine, *Common Sense*

Finding and keeping the right people is one of the most important aspects of a first line manager's job. Without the right people, performing jobs to which they are well suited, the organization would slowly grind to a halt.

You are in the best position to match suitable people to the work for which you are responsible. However, this cannot be done purely by instinct – you need to have a clear understanding of the purpose of the job, how it fits into the organization, and what kind of person might be best suited to do the work. Then you need to become very good at assessing who, among the job applicants, is most likely to fit in and perform the job well, ensuring job satisfaction for the individual and a productive and happy worker for the organization.

3.1 Objectives

When you have completed this workbook, you will be better able to:

- take part in the recruitment and selection process;
- prepare for interviews;
- plan, prepare and carry out an effective selection interview;
- assess the information you obtain during an interview;
- plan and implement good induction schemes for your workteam;
- design and implement policies related to retaining staff.

4 Activity planner

The following Activities require some planning so you may want to look at these now.

Activity 9   Asks you to think about personnel requirements in your organization.

Activity 28   Looks at the way new staff are selected (shortlisted, interviewed and notifed) in your organization.

Activity 43   Encourages you to consider ongoing development and training for your team.

Portfolio of evidence

Some or all of these Activities may provide the basis of evidence for your S/NVQ portfolio. All Portfolio Activities and the Work-based assignment are signposted with this icon.

The icon states the elements to which the Portfolio Activities and Work-based assignment relate.

The Work-based assignment (on page 64) involves assessing the recruitment process in your organization. It will help you meet some of the performance criteria from element C7.1, Contribute to identifying personnel requirements and element C7.2, Contribute to selecting required personnel.

Session A Filling a vacancy

Recruiting a new individual is a chance to shift the balance of the company as a whole, so it is important that you bear in mind where you are trying to take the company.

John Harvey-Jones

1 Introduction

Vacancies arise in all sorts of different ways. A new department may be set up as the result of expansion, duties may be re-allocated, or an existing team member may retire, move house or find another job.

We'll begin this session by discussing how to begin the process of recruiting someone. Then we'll go on to look in more detail at how to get the right person for the job.

2 A vacancy exists . . .

Let's begin by considering a typical situation. A member of the workteam leaves so a vacancy arises. Or does it? In our examination of the whole question of recruiting people, we need to start one step back from there and think hard about that possible vacancy.

■ Charmian is the manager of a small pharmaceutical company which sells and markets a number of drugs in the UK. She has a team of ten sales representatives working from home and a staff of three based in the office. Gemma is her full-time PA and Louise and Anna work part time as marketing assistants for the sales team, arranging appointments, sending out literature and so on.

Gemma hands in her notice. Charmian immediately calls her head office in the US to let them know that she will advertise for a new PA. But she is told that the head count in the UK office is being looked into and for the moment she will have to manage with her two part-time staff.

Charmian is livid. So are Louise and Anna who quickly realize that they will be expected to carry out Gemma's duties once she leaves. How are they going to manage?

I

Louise and Anna are expected do the PA work as well as their normal jobs and both put in extra hours in a week to keep on top of things. Anna finds that she enjoys the variety of her work and suggests to Charmian that she could take on full-time work and combine the part-time marketing assistant's post with part-time PA work. Charmian had always thought that her PA's post had to be full time, but since Gemma left she has been doing some of the work herself and agrees that it could be a part-time post.

The head of human resources in the US takes some time to agree to the extra half member of staff, but is pleased that she has succeeded in reducing the head count in the UK in the medium term.

You may have had a similar experience. If so, you and your team will have had to reorganize yourselves to get the jobs done – just as a soccer team has to reorganize if one player gets sent off. Some or all of your team members may have to extend their responsibilities to fill the gap. You may find that this makes your team more efficient and cohesive.

It's also worth finding out whether the vacancy can be filled from elsewhere in the organization. If there's a ban on recruitment, it could be that other parts of the organization are being restructured, and you may be able to save someone else from being made redundant.

> '*Haste in every business brings failure.*'
>
> Herodotus, *The Histories* book VII, ch. 10

So when someone leaves, consider all the options before you assume that you'll just get someone else appointed to fill the vacant post.

3 Starting the recruitment and selection process

Now let us turn our attention to selecting a new permanent employee from outside the organization.

We begin with certain assumptions:

- a vacancy does exist;
- it cannot be filled from within the organization;
- your team can't be reorganized to cover the gap in the medium to long term;
- the organization will authorize the request to take on a new employee.

The first step of the recruitment process is to find out your organization's policies and procedures. If your organization has a human resources department, it will guide management in the recruitment and selection of new employees. HRD professionals are able to advise on employment law, the best places to advertise, interviewing techniques and so on, and ensure that the organization's human resources policies and procedures are followed.

If you work for a smaller organization you may have to do the whole job yourself. Even then, the recruitment policy must still be applied and you may have recognized procedures to follow.

4 Analysing the job

The second step in the process is to analyse the vacancy to be filled.

■ Jamie Keeler came to the conclusion that his team could not continue to cope without further help. When Damion had retired six months earlier, Jamie's manager had persuaded him to try to operate without a replacement. Although the team had responded well, the workload was now increasing and substantial new sales orders seemed to justify the cost of an extra person.

Jamie went to see his manager, who agreed, 'But I will need to know exactly what this person will do, Jamie. Things have moved on a bit since Damion retired, so there's no point in basing the new post on his job description.'

Back at his office, Jamie sat down with a blank sheet of paper.

Replacing someone who has left, or creating a new vacancy, is an expensive business. Some of the questions you should ask are as follows.

■ Does the vacancy really exist?
■ What is the nature of the job?

Job analysis answers both these questions. We must begin by asking a few basic questions.

■ What is the purpose of the post?
■ What are the performance standards that we are looking for?
■ What special contribution does the post make to the overall effectiveness of the organization?
■ What would happen if the post were not filled?
■ Does the post justify its level in terms of seniority or grading?
■ Will the post continue to exist in the future? (If yes, for how long?)

Activity 1

15 mins

It might be uncomfortable to try to answer these six questions about your own job! Instead, take a look at a job carried out by one of your workteam. Be careful not to take anything for granted. The fact that things have always been done a certain way does not mean that they should stay that way.

_____

_____

_____

_____

_____

_____

If you found Activity 1 difficult, one useful approach is to use the 'critical examination' technique. Ask yourself the following questions.

- **What** has to be done?
- **How** is it done?
- **When** is it done?
- **Where** is it done?
- **Who** does it?
- **Why** is it done?

If you can find no reasons why it is done, or only weak ones, you are probably on to something! Go back and ask some slightly different questions:

- **What else** could be done?
- **How else** could it be done?
- **When else** could it be done?
- **Where else** could it be done?
- **Who else** could do it?

By doing this you will have thought about the job in a much deeper way than before.

Perhaps you have proved to yourself that the job really does have to be done as before by a certain kind of person with skills and characteristics very similar to those of the previous job holder.

On the other hand, perhaps you identified that a change is needed and the job could be split, be done in a different way, or be done by someone on a different grade. Maybe the job was, or soon will be, unnecessary. In this case, you could well consider not filling it at all. Indeed, in the current 'slim-line' climate, this is one way of improving efficiency.

Once you've decided what the job is about, you need to write a job description and a person specification to match.

5 Job descriptions

In any well run organization, every employee should have a job description, listing their duties and responsibilities.

We are concerned here with the part you can play in human resource management. Getting your own and your workteam's job descriptions right is an important part of this aspect of management.

Even if the organization you work for is a large one with HRD specialists, you remain the expert about how work is done in your particular area, and so your knowledge is vital in drawing up the job descriptions in your department – and perhaps even more important in keeping them up to date as jobs change and new practices are introduced.

Let's look at a couple of examples of job descriptions first.

Job Description 1	
Job title:	Printing machine operator
Department:	Advertising section
Purpose:	Prepares and operates various types of printing equipment to produce advertising documents to the required standards of finish.
Main tasks:	1 Sets up types of varying size.
	2 Sets up and operates various printing machines and ancillary equipment.
	3 Prints plates from suitable negatives.
	4 Uses camera to photograph artwork for reproduction.
	5 Processes film using suitable methods and darkroom equipment.
	6 Records job requirements and material used.
	7 Maintains and cleans machines.
Areas of difficulty:	Ensuring accuracy in setting type and laying out of work.
	Using different types of equipment to carry out a variety of printing requirements.
Environment:	Warm, well lit. Clean but some use of chemicals in darkroom.

Another example of a job description, using different headings but designed with the same purpose in mind, is as follows:

Job Description 2	
Job title:	Catering assistant
Reporting to:	Catering supervisor
Function:	Catering assistants are required to carry out general kitchen work under the direction of the catering supervisor, including cooking and cleaning, and to serve food to company staff at meal times.
Duties:	(a) To prepare vegetables prior to cooking.
	(b) To prepare and mix ingredients for pies, cakes and other dishes, according to recipes provided.
	(c) To attend to food being cooked on hot plates and in ovens.
	(d) To clean working surfaces and utensils, using equipment provided.
	(e) To serve dishes to company staff in the canteen servery.
	(f) To maintain high standards of hygiene at all times.
Working conditions:	Normal kitchen environment. Hours as specified on letter of appointment. Some overtime possible.

A job description gives an overall picture of the job function, and a list of duties to be performed. It provides potential job holders with a good understanding of what they are expected to do. It is also a reference document in case of dispute.

Activity 2

Take a close look at your own job description and see whether it covers the six points listed below. Summarize what it says according to these points. If you don't have a job description, write a brief one now with reference to the six points. This Activity should make you think quite hard about what you actually do.

1 Title of post

2 To whom accountable

3 For what tasks

    a directly responsible
    b indirectly responsible

4 Resources controlled

    a human (staff)
    b financial (budgets, value of output)
    c physical (plant and equipment)

5 Liaison links

    a internal
    b external

6 Limits to authority

> **EXTENSION I**
> Look at C. Goodworth's book *Effective Interviewing*, 'Use — and be familiar with — the job specification. Remember, like it or not, it is the blueprint of the successful candidate.'

You may have found that your existing job description no longer reflects what you do and you may feel it needs updating now. You should discuss this with your manager and HRD.

Activity 3

Now try your hand at sketching out a job description for the job you looked at in Activity 1. Do this on a separate sheet of paper using the headings given below. Do this activity without referring to an actual job description that may already exist for this post.

Job title

Function

Duties

Working conditions

You may have found this task really makes you think about what the job actually consists of. For a newly created job, it may be harder. Obviously the question then becomes: 'What exactly do I want the new person to do?'

7

6 Person specifications

The person or employee specification is intended to portray the sort of person we would ideally like to fill the post.

Activity 4

3 mins

Why do you think it is useful to have a person specification as well as a job description?

_____

_____

_____

The main value of a person specification is that it enables us to compare applicants for the job against an ideal, rather than simply comparing one applicant with another. Both the job description and the person specification provide a fixed standard – something very important where subjective judgements are involved.

Once the job description is drawn up, we know the shape and size of the 'hole'. Now for the 'peg'. We need to convert our picture of the job into a pen portrait of the ideal person to fill it.

Activity 5

4 mins

List at least four requirements you would expect to find in a person specification which describes 'the ideal candidate'. Here are two to get you started:

Standard of education expected.

Previous experience required.

_____

_____

_____

_____

You might have written down any of the following:

- Knowledge required
- Experience required
- Standard of education and academic qualifications
- Other qualifications (driving licence, first aid certificates)
- Physical abilities/disabilities (manual dexterity, strength, suitability for a person with disabilities)
- Specific skills (keyboard skills)
- Ability to communicate
- Social skills
- Appearance (someone dealing with the public may be expected to dress smartly).

We can group these points under three main headings:

6.1 Knowledge and skill

What does the job holder need to know to be able to do the job? This knowledge may include how to use certain machinery, handle certain materials or follow certain procedures. What skills are required to do the job? For instance: manual dexterity, ability to work with figures.

6.2 Qualifications and experience

Are any formal qualifications required? What occupational training and experience should the job holder already have?

6.3 Personal factors

What sort of person will best fit into the existing workteam? Is there an upper or lower age limit? Should the job holder have above-average strength? Might any domestic circumstances be important: for example, no shift work?

Here is a person specification for the catering assistant post you looked at in Job description 2. Together the two documents should give us a job specification and could provide details of what the job involved and the sort of person required to do it.

Post of catering assistant: person specification

Knowledge required:	Must know the basics of food preparation and cookery.
Experience required:	Ideally will have worked in similar job elsewhere.
Appearance:	Neat, clean appearance. (Overalls provided.)
Standard of education:	Must be able to read.
Academic qualifications:	City and Guilds General Catering desirable.
Physical abilities:	Must be capable of lifting and carrying heavy pans. Not suitable for person in wheelchair, owing to height of surfaces, etc.
Specific skills:	None required. Training will be given where necessary.
Ability to communicate:	Must be able to communicate verbally with other staff and with canteen customers.
Social skills:	Must be able to work as part of team in confined kitchen atmosphere, and to get on well with other employees when serving in canteen.

You will notice that in some places this person specification uses the words 'must' and at other points 'ideally' or 'desirable'. In other words, some requirements are essential, while others are desirable. Some person specifications make this distinction clear in the way they are laid out – there may be a column for essential points and another column for desirable points.

Although we have a clear idea of the ideal candidate, we acknowledge the fact that we may have to settle for something less. So we set certain minimum requirements, and hope to find someone who has qualities, skills or experience above these minimum levels. This is being realistic, not pessimistic.

Activity 6

10 mins

Draw up a person specification based on the job description which you prepared in Activity 3. You need only use the headings from the list below that are appropriate to the job.

Knowledge required

Experience required

Standard of education

Academic qualifications

Other qualifications

Physical abilities/disabilities

Specific skills

Ability to communicate

Social skills

Appearance.

'The process of selection must be one of the most important exercises in the business calendar.'

John Harvey-Jones

7 Job specification

The job description and the person specification together form the job specification. This is a complete blueprint of the job itself and the person required to do the job.

Activity 7

5 mins

Why is it important not to understate the requirements of a job specification?

_____

_____

Why is it important not to overstate the requirements of a job specification?

_____

_____

If we understate what is required the new job holder is unlikely to be effective. If we overstate the requirements, we run the risk of recruiting someone who will quickly lose interest and motivation to do the job.

8 Getting approval

The next step in the process of filling a vacancy should be an obvious one: it is concerned with obtaining the authorization to recruit a new employee.

Usually only the more senior managers in the organization have the authority to spend money and resources on recruiting new staff. A line manager usually has to persuade their manager (who in turn may need to persuade someone higher up) that this expense can be justified.

Starting the process of hiring somebody is difficult to justify unless the job has first been clearly defined and all other avenues and options have been explored.

9 Attracting the applicants

We should now have a clear idea about the kind of 'peg' required for the 'hole' in question, so we can move on to the stage of searching for our ideal employee. Will we find him or her inside or outside the organization? How are we likely to make contact?

To recruit internally we could do the following:

- Put up notices on staff notice-boards.
- Circulate to all departments a regular 'broadsheet' of jobs available.
- Run the entire payroll through the computer to see if anybody in the organization already fits the bill.

The range of methods to recruit new people from outside the organization may include:

- advertising in a national newspaper;
- advertising in trade magazines;
- advertising in a local newspaper;
- advertising on commercial radio;
- sending round leaflets to houses in the local area;
- placing the vacancy with one or more recruitment agencies.

If you are put in a position where you have to make the decision yourself, remember that many of these methods can be very expensive indeed, particularly advertising nationally. In general, more highly paid jobs are likely to appeal to people from a wider geographical area and warrant advertisements in national or regional papers, while jobs requiring less experience and paying less are more likely to attract local people and can be advertised in the local media.

Recruitment agencies only charge you when a suitable candidate is found – but then the costs can be very high.

It is important to make clear to potential applicants what you want them to do, for example, write a letter of application, send in a CV (curriculum vitae), telephone for further details. And it's crucial to give a contact address or telephone number.

Once you have advertised, you may receive dozens or even hundreds of replies. You need to give some thought as to how the applicants will be dealt with. Most people like to hear something, one way or another, so even if you decide to reject people without offering an interview, it's essential to write a brief letter saying that this is the case.

We will look in more detail at the next stages of the process – shortlisting and interviewing – in Session B.

10 Employment law

Before we go any further, there are two pieces of employment law that you should be aware of regarding recruitment.

10.1 The Race Relations Act 1976

This act prohibits any discrimination on the grounds of colour, race or ethnic or national origin. The Race Relations Act 1976 established the Commission for Racial Equality, which is responsible for promoting the objectives of the Act. It also has powers to investigate discriminatory practices, and advises the Government on ways to improve legislation. Individuals who believe they have been discriminated against can take their case to an industrial tribunal.

10.2 The Sex Discrimination Act 1975

This Act makes discrimination on the grounds of sex or marriage unlawful. The Equal Opportunities Commission was set up to promote the objectives of both this Act and the Equal Pay Act 1970. Again, anyone who feels discriminated against may go to an industrial tribunal.

There are certain exceptions to this Act for positions where the sex of a person employed is genuinely a necessary qualification for the job, for example, the role of a man in a theatre production.

There are other Acts and points of law which affect employment of people. Your human resources department will know about them. If you would like to go into the subject further, refer to the study links section at the beginning of the unit.

Activity 8

2 mins

What do you think you can you do to make sure that these two laws are upheld when you are filling vacancies?

_____

_____

_____

Many organizations have a policy that all personnel advertisements indicate that they are an equal opportunities employer. It will be important, when considering the kinds of questions you might ask at interview, not to include questions which could be construed as being racist or sexist, or to make assumptions based on sex or race, such as that a young woman will be going off to have a baby as soon as she is trained up to the job.

Portfolio of evidence C7.1

Activity 9

30 mins

This Activity may provide the basis of possible acceptable evidence for your S/NVQ portfolio. If you are intending to take this course of action, it might be better for you to write your answers on separate sheets of paper.

1   In your place of work imagine that you are able to create a new post or substantially change an existing post. Consider the needs of the organization and list what advantages and disadvantages there would be in creating this new post or changing the existing one. Take into account the work objectives of the team/department and any constraints. Show how you have completed this critical appraisal process.

2   Assuming the post is to be advertised, design a job description and person specification.

3   Collect together any organizational policy documents that relate to employment and identify who needs to be informed of decisions or intentions to recruit a new member of staff. Is there any part of the documentation that you need to learn more about? If so, make a list of learning objectives for yourself to achieve and a plan to achieve them. Make sure you take into account legal requirements and say how you have done this.

14

Self-assessment 1

1 Complete the following five sentences with the suitable word or words chosen from the list.

procedures   document   reference   person
description   policies   job   specification

a The first step in the process of filling a vacancy is to find out about your

organization's _____ and _____.

b A _____ _____ sets out the responsibilities and tasks of

an employee.

c A job specification consists of a job description and a _____

_____ .

d In cases of dispute, a job description can be a useful _____

_____ .

2 What headings might you use in a person specification?

3 What questions do you need to ask yourself when beginning to draw up a job description?

4 Before advertising for new employees, what is it essential for you to do?

5 What information should be included in the job advertisement to attract the right kind of people to apply?

6 Which two pieces of legislation are particularly relevant when filling vacancies?

Answers to these questions can be found on pages 73–4.

11 Summary

- When a vacancy arises, you will need to analyse the job by asking:

  - What is the purpose of the post?
  - What performance standards are required?
  - How does this post contribute to the overall effectiveness of the organization?

- You will then need to prepare a Job Specification consisting of a job description and person specification. A job description helps both managers and job holders to be clear about what is expected:

  - what has to be done
  - how the job is done
  - when it is done
  - where it is done.

- The person specification considers:

  - education and qualifications
  - personal characteristics
  - skills and experience.

- Once you have gained approval to fill the new post, you will need to attract the best possible applicants, which may be the responsibility of the human resources department. It is crucial to remember relevant legislation covering employment, particularly the Race Relations Act and the Sex Discrimination Act.

Session B Making the right choice

No matter how systematised selection procedures are, it seems to me that the ability to assess the ultimate potential of individuals after a relatively short exposure to them is a gift.

Sir John Harvey-Jones, *All Together Now*

1 Introduction

Selecting the right person for the job is one of the hardest decisions you may have to make. You can't really get to know how well someone will perform until they've worked in your team for some time. Yet the only opportunity you usually have to choose between applicants for a job is an hour or so in an interview room.

Interviewing has its drawbacks, and few would claim that it is a completely reliable way to ensure that the right person gets the job. Nevertheless, when it is carried out competently, it is still one of the best methods of assessing people.

Some organizations use techniques in addition to interviewing, which are often carried out by professionals in the field. These might include psychological testing (designed to determine whether the person has the right 'mental make-up' for the job), practical skills tests or the use of assessment centres to determine people's suitability for jobs. But even when such methods are used, nearly everyone also carries out an interview.

In this session we examine the interview, how to prepare for it and how to assess the candidates afterwards.

2 Why do we interview?

'... it is important to be clear about what one is trying to do at the interviewing stage. The object of the exercise is to learn as much about the character, values and potential of the person as possible in a very limited period and in artificial circumstances. In a way the whole thing is a bit like a detective story, where you are looking for elusive clues to follow up, which will reveal more of the plot.'

Sir John Harvey-Jones, *All Together Now*

Activity 10

5 mins

EXTENSION 1
C. Goodworth's book *Effective Interviewing* gives a good summary of the purpose of a job selection interview:

'A face-to-face interview is well justified in terms of the human relations value involved; its purpose is to carry out a comprehensive and background investigation — to seek out and verify the facts of past achievement and failure. The name of the interviewing game is perception and prediction.'

What is the main purpose of the job interview?

_____

_____

_____

_____

You might have said:

■ to find out whether the applicant is suitable for the job;
■ to find out if the job is suitable for the applicant;
■ to assess the applicant;
■ to receive information about the applicant, and to give information about the organization.

Here's one definition of a job interview: it is designed to determine the facts about a candidate in terms of knowledge, experience, past achievements and failures, to ascertain whether they are likely to do a specified job well.

3 Preparing for the interview

The interview will be a crucial time for you and the candidates. It is worth making the time and effort to prepare well for this important event.

3.1 Shortlisting for interviews

The first thing to do is to sort out which applicants are likely to be suitable. This process is known as shortlisting.

Some organizations use standard application forms when inviting people to apply for jobs, which makes it easier to compare applicants. The usual alternative to the application form is a letter, accompanied by a CV which lists the employment history and personal details of the applicant. The CVs received will be in a variety of formats, styles and presentations, making the selection process more difficult.

3.2 Interpreting the applications

Let's work out some useful tips for shortlisting applicants.

Look at the following checklist, which was compiled from a job specification, and the application forms received for the position of secretary.

Requirement	Name of applicant						
	Smith	Brown	Sanchez	Heinz	Wester	Peterson	Goldstein
Shorthand speed: min. 80 wpm	100	85	130	65	90	80	85
Typing speed: should be >30 wpm	35	40	45	40	25	35	40
Office experience: min. 2 years	1	3	8	6	4	2	5

The job was advertised with three criteria for applicants listed:

■ a shorthand speed of at least 80 words per minute or above;
■ a typing speed of 30 words per minute or above;
■ a minimum of two years' office experience.

Activity 11

Which names would you eliminate from the checklist and why?

_____

_____

_____

_____

You could eliminate Heinz because of the slow shorthand, Wester because of the slow typing, Smith because of insufficient experience, and Sanchez, who seems, on the evidence of his qualifications and experience, to be over-qualified for the job.

If your advertisement is vague, you may get both under- and over-qualified applicants. Someone who is over-qualified may be just as much a misfit in a job as someone who is under-qualified.

If all applicants have filled out their application forms fully and correctly, you may find yourself in the lucky position of having all the information you need about your prospective recruits. This is a rare situation! But you are likely to find things which aren't clear and need expanding. Make a note at this point on each application form of the points you will need to query.

Activity 12

3 mins

Why should you be wary of job titles?

_____

_____

_____

Job titles can be misleading. If someone describes themselves as a senior operator, what does that signify? Your organization may use the same term, but mean something quite different. Many organizations use rather grand titles. For example, a salesperson may be called a sales manager to make them sound more important.

3.3 Setting up the interviews

The interview is the central core of the recruitment process but, as we have already seen, a lot of important decision-making goes on before you get that far. Similarly, the interview itself requires some effective organization if it is to be successful.

Activity 13

4 mins

Describe your idea of a perfect interview room.

_____

_____

_____

You may have said:

- private;
- free from interruptions;
- comfortably warm;

20

- with comfortable (upright) seating;
- quiet;
- with a table to write on.

Ideally, you shouldn't put a barrier such as a desk between you and the interviewee. Sitting around a table often seems more natural than having two chairs in the middle of a room, but it is better to sit at right angles to the interviewee than directly opposite. It is also better if all the seating is the same height, so that interviewer and interviewee can speak on equal terms.

4 The functions of the interviewer

The success of an interview, both in terms of enabling interviewees to perform well and employers to make a good appointment, depends largely on the effectiveness of the interviewer.

Activity 14

3 mins

Pick out the three most important functions of an interviewer:

a To describe the job to the interviewee.
b To ask questions.
c To prompt candidates into talking about themselves.
d To explain about the job.
e To listen.
f To keep interviewees on their toes.
g To put interviewees at their ease.
h To pressurize interviewees into revealing the truth about themselves.

_____

_____

_____

The three most important functions of an interviewer are to:

- put interviewees at their ease;
- prompt interviewees into talking about themselves;
- listen.

The reasons should be quite obvious. What an interviewer is trying to establish is whether the interviewee can do the job and whether they have the personality that will fit in with the rest of the team. This can only be done if the candidate speaks freely and openly about past experience, achievements, ambitions, likes, dislikes and so on.

21

So you need to decide what you want to find out from each candidate. You don't want to wait until the interviews start and then have to search for appropriate questions. This means going through the job specification and all the applications carefully, and picking up on the queries you had already marked. You might decide to ask each candidate the same questions, so that you can compare the replies. But you have to be ready to vary your line of questioning, depending on the replies.

5 Interview format

We can think about the interview as having several stages:

Stage 1: Introduction and opening remarks.
Stage 2: The interviewer explaining what the job is about, and what the organization does.
Stage 3: Some direct questions, to confirm facts given on the application form.
Stage 4: The main part of the interview to establish the background, experience and ability of the candidate.
Stage 5: A request for the interviewee to ask questions.
Stage 6: Rounding off the interview, with the interviewer summarizing the position and stating what the next step is.
Stage 7: Showing the interviewee around the workplace (if appropriate).

You may find it helpful to draw up a standard checklist of questions and issues for each stage – this will help you focus on what needs to be done at any one time.

6 Welcoming the interviewees

Every organization depends a great deal on its image. If a visitor's first impression is of scruffy offices and unenthusiastic staff, the organization's business will ultimately suffer, no matter how good its products are.

So make sure that:

■ each interviewee's first contact on arrival is courteous and friendly;
■ the receptionist knows who to expect, and when they're arriving;
■ the waiting place is comfortable and bright, preferably with up-to-date literature;
■ the waiting time is kept to a minimum.

Part of your task as an interviewer should be to ensure that:

■ you show the interviewee that you respect them;
■ you let the interviewee know that you are taking the interview seriously.

Activity 15

3 mins

What do you think would be a good way of starting the interview?

_____

_____

_____

_____

One good way would be to begin by starting off with a few 'soft' questions to get them talking before the interview proper begins. Interviewees will only speak freely if they are at their ease. You could then move on by saying, 'I'll start by telling you about the organization and the job? After that, you can tell me more about yourself. Then I'll try to answer any questions you may have.'

Two lessons can be learned here:

■ think about the kind of response you want before you ask a question;
■ ask open questions.

Let's go on to look at questions in more detail.

7 Asking questions

The purpose of questioning is to prompt the interviewee into providing information. This information must be sufficient to allow the interviewer to judge the suitability of the interviewee for the job.

7.1 Open questions

EXTENSION 2
K. J. Murphy, in his book *Management by Effective Listening*, sums up the task of the job selection interviewer very neatly: 'Keep the door of communication open and, one way or the other, the candidate is sure to talk through it.'

Open questions are designed to allow the interviewees to describe, in their own words, the subject under consideration.

A question beginning: 'Tell me about . . .' followed by some aspect of the interviewee's experience, or some other matter, is a good open question.

Other open questions begin with the words what/why/where/how/which/when. They are all good starter words, but they don't provide a magic formula. You have to put some thought behind what you are asking. For example, questions such as 'What is your name?' and 'Where do you live?' are direct questions.

The following are also open questions:

'Do you have any suggestions as to how . . .?'

'Can you give me an idea of the sort of problems you met when . . .?'

'Could you summarize the situation for me?'

Activity 16

Read the following few minutes of an interview. What is the interviewer doing quite successfully?

Interviewer: Why did you decide to leave Grundy's?

Interviewee: I had been doing the same job for two years, and I realized that I was missing the contact with people I used to have. I suppose you could say it was job satisfaction – or lack of it.

Interviewer: When you left and went to Brown & Smithson, was that more interesting? Can you expand on that job a bit for me?

Interviewee: Although I was still working in a similar office, the position I had in Brown & Smithson was much more to do with the problems that customers were having. It meant I wasn't shut away with just my files for company.

Interviewer: What exactly was that job? Tell me more about it.

_____

_____

_____

You have probably said that the interviewer is using questions as prompts. He is also taking the candidate's answers on the application form as a starting point, and is phrasing his questions according to the answers of the previous question.

7.2 Getting the interviewee to talk

You will want to know if the interviewee is experienced enough. How can you tell? The application form should tell you a great deal, but what you need to be sure of now is that what is written down is true.

Activity 17

3 mins

If an interviewee says they have line management experience, how would you set about finding out whether they are telling the truth?

_____

_____

_____

_____

The approach you could start with is to ask more about what it's like to be a supervisor. If they are vague in their reply, you might put a question like: 'How do you cope when several members of your team are away at the same time?' Vague replies will tell you that all is not what it seems. But there's no point in confrontation or accusation.

EXTENSION 2
To quote Murphy once more: 'Interrupting or finishing statements for the candidate is like talking to yourself: you feel good but learn nothing.'

What if the interviewee tries to say too much, and wanders from the point? A good interviewer interrupts as little as possible but sometimes a talkative interviewee may have to be interrupted. It's best not to do this in the middle of a sentence, but to wait until there's a slight pause. Then phrases like the following can be used: 'Good. That gives me some background information. Could you now be more specific about . . .' or 'That's very interesting. I'd like now to move on to . . .'

8 Keeping to a natural sequence

This sounds like common sense but, given that interviewer and interviewee are probably a bit on edge, it is something which can go awry.

Activity 18

3 mins

Read the following excerpt from a job interview.

Interviewer: Tell me about your experience in the nursery. What did you do there?

Interviewee: Well, I was there for two and a half years. I started with virtually no experience of young children, but the people there were extremely helpful. By the end, I was more or less running the nursery.

Interviewer: What qualifications did you get when you left school?

Interviewee: I got four 'O' levels in . . .

Interviewer: Why did you go to work in a shop in Shipton?

Interviewee: That was a long time before the nursery work. My husband at the time was travelling a lot, and I took the job in the shop because I found I had a lot of spare time and needed to . . .

Interviewer: What are your hobbies, Jane?

Interviewee: I read a lot, and I play tennis. I spend a lot of my spare time with handicapped people.

Interviewer: Let's go back to the nursery work . . .

Comment on the way this interviewer is putting the questions.

_____

_____

_____

You have probably said that the interviewer interrupted on a couple of occasions and did not seem to put the questions in any logical sequence.

This kind of questioning, usually caused by a lack of concentration on the part of the interviewer, comes over like some kind of 'third-degree' interrogation. It's sensible to ask questions in a natural sequence. This doesn't always have to be a strict chronological order, but a good interviewer will avoid confusing the interviewee by picking on subjects at random.

Activity 19

If you want to find out more about an interviewee's last job, which of the following questions is most likely to prompt them into talking further?

- ■ 'What did you do in your last job?' ☐
- ■ 'Can you tell me about your last job?' ☐
- ■ 'This last job you did – interesting, was it?' ☐

The second one is the best kind of question to ask at an interview. It is an open question and you have effectively asked the interviewee to describe the previous job, in their own words. The first one is a direct question. All you will do is establish a fact that should already be on the application form. Direct questions tend to get direct replies. The third one is a leading question. You have emphasized one aspect of the work – how interesting it was. A leading question puts words in the mouth of the person being questioned. You are likely to get the reply: 'Yes, it was interesting.' It doesn't get you much further.

Activity 20

If, in the middle of an interview, you realize that the interviewee is clearly not suitable for the position, what could you say?

_____

_____

_____

The answer to this question depends on how convinced you are about the situation. If you are absolutely certain that the interviewee won't fill the bill, this should be clear to the interviewee as well.

You could say something like: 'It seems from what you have told me that you have not got the amount of experience that my company is demanding for this job. Do you agree with that, or is there anything more you'd like to add?' If they disagree, then give them a further opportunity to prove you wrong. Sooner or later you may have to close the interview by saying something like: 'Well, I'd like to thank you for coming here today and found what you had to say very interesting. I must be frank with you though; your experience and training is not adequate for the position we have to fill . . .'

If you aren't sure, though, it is better to complete the interview as you may discover that your initial assessment was wrong.

27

9 Taking notes

It may seem altogether too much to be expected to take notes as well as listen and ask a logical sequence of questions. You may also feel that it looks rather rude if you spend more than a few seconds writing. But note-taking is an important activity for an interviewer.

Activity 21

3 mins

Why do you think note-taking is important at an interview?

_____

_____

You may have said that it reminds you of what was said, what the interviewee was like, what you thought of each person, and so on. You will find this essential if you are holding several interviews on the same day as it's always difficult to remember one particular interview after you've conducted several.

What sort of notes should be taken? There may be times when you feel that your notes must be fairly comprehensive and detailed. In many cases, though, just a line or two will suffice. The important thing is to make notes while the interviewee's details are still fresh in your mind – during the interview or after and before you see the next interviewee. It's a good idea to tell the interviewee that you are going to make notes.

10 Rounding off the interview

The best interviews will make good use of everybody's time. It is terrible to be in a position where the interview lingers on because no one seems to know how to close it.

How can the interviewer be sure that important facts will not be forgotten? One way is for the interviewer to give a summary of what has taken place. You could say: 'I've been taking notes of all that you've told me. Perhaps I could now briefly summarize. If I miss out anything important, please let me know.'

11 Assessing the candidates

How do you compare one interviewee with another? Unless you adopt a systematic approach, it can be very difficult.

Activity 22

3 mins

Read the following account. How might you avoid the kind of difficulty described above?

■ I was interviewing for a PA. The first candidate was quite impressive. I was satisfied that they would fit in well with the team and seemed to have the right kind of experience. Of course, I couldn't offer the job at this point, as I had four other candidates to see.

The second interviewee was also very good. She also seemed to be well qualified to do the job and I thought she had a very pleasant personality. Just as I was wondering how to choose between the two, the next interview began. This candidate turned out to have rather special experience which could be extremely useful.

At the end of the five interviews, I'd picked out four people who I felt were very good. I hadn't planned on holding second interviews and I couldn't remember exactly who had said what.

_____

_____

_____

_____

_____

You may have suggested that it would be a good idea to draw up a checklist by referring to the job specification, and to fill it in for each candidate.

Once you have made a decision about appointing someone to a job, it is likely to be a long time before you know whether the selection was the right one. If your decision was a good one, the new member of staff will perform well. If it was a bad one, they will perform badly. Selecting a bad candidate is not the only possible mistake, though. The other kind of wrong decision you might make is to reject the best candidate. How can you maximize your chances of getting it right?

Here are some common methods for comparing candidates.

11.1 A ranking method

One means of comparing candidates is to rank them against specified attributes. For example, before interviewing five interviewees for the position of PA, you list a number of qualities to be assessed: teamwork, qualifications, amount of experience, and so on. After the interviews, you would rank the candidates in order, against each desired quality, as shown below:

Rank	Teamwork	Qualifications	Experience
1	Hazel	Footsore	Hazel
2	Prince	Caterham	Trinder
3	Footsore	Hazel	Prince
4	Caterham	Trinder	Footsore
5	Trinder	Prince	Caterham

Activity 23

3 mins

Can you think of any disadvantages of this system?

_____

_____

You may have said that you will have to decide how important each quality is in the overall assessment. If one candidate is outstanding, and comes near the top of every list, there is less difficulty, of course.

The other disadvantage is that the assessment cannot be made until all candidates have been seen. If interviews are spread out over more than one day, it may be difficult to remember what particular interviewees said exactly, let alone how good they were in comparison with another.

One compromise solution to this problem would be to compare the first candidate with the second, for each quality, and then to ask: 'Is the third candidate better than either of the other two?' This process would then have to be repeated for each candidate.

You may agree that the ranking system, on its own, is not an ideal one.

11.2 A scoring system

Another method of assessing prospective employees is to make a list of key points and give each person a mark between 1 and 5 for each point.

Before the interview, draw up your list of key points by deciding which factors about the job are important. The list may look something like this for the post of telephone sales assistant.

Name _____

Item	Key factors	Score	Comments
Experience:	Should have done this kind of work before		
Verbal skills:	Must be able to talk clearly, and have a pleasant voice		
Telephone manner:	(Simulated test)		
Personality:	Bright, outgoing personality required		
Salary required:			
Availability:	Should be able to start within two weeks		
Overall impression:			

A score for each category should have a specific meaning. For instance, 'verbal skills' might be classified as follows:

1	2	3	4	5
Inarticulate. Very poor projection and vocabulary.	Poor voice quality, projection and vocabulary.	Average voice, reasonably well put over. Fair vocabulary.	Generally a good voice with no real problems. Good vocabulary.	Excellent, well projected, with pleasing effects. Very good vocabulary.

Other categories would be classified in the same way. A simpler scale for all categories is often used:

1	2	3	4	5
Unsatisfactory	Poor	Average	Good	Excellent

No system is perfect and we are all liable to give higher scores to those candidates we take a liking to than to those we don't. It is not easy to be totally objective about assessment.

This is particularly true of personality. It is important to be aware of your own prejudices and try to be as objective as possible by continually bearing the job description and person specification in mind and thinking about the kind of person who will do a good job, work well with the whole team and contribute to the team effort.

There are several common pitfalls for assessors. It is a common failing for an assessor to be kind or lenient, and not to mark any candidate low in a grading system. The result, of course, is that the task of deciding the best candidate becomes even harder.

'There are a surprisingly large number of people who seem to be interview stars, but in practice are ineffectual.'

John Harvey-Jones
All Together Now

There can also be a tendency for an assessor to give too little thought when marking candidates against a scale. This is particularly true when a number of candidates must be seen. It requires more effort to spend a few minutes giving careful consideration to each item for each candidate.

Another pitfall is what is called the 'halo effect'. This is illustrated in the next acitivity.

Activity 24

2 mins

You are interviewing two candidates for a job where personality is not all that important. You find you get on really well with the first person. The next candidate is a little harder to get along with, but is much better qualified for the job than the first interviewee. Who would you choose, and why?

_____

_____

Because of the wording of this leading question, you probably would not have hesitated in choosing the second candidate. In real-life situations, though, it is very easy to be over-enthusiastic about a candidate you get on well with, and overlook any observed faults.

11.3 Shortlisting

Another technique which is often used to select people for jobs is known as 'shortlisting'. This is generally done on the basis of the information contained in application forms. The names of people whose experience seems to match the job description and whose qualifications seem to match the person specification are written down on a shortlist of potential interviewees. This is a way of reducing the number of people to interview by selecting only the most likely candidates.

12 Following up the interview

All candidates should be able to provide the names of referees who will be able to back up claims of experience and performance. One of these referees should be the person's present or previous employer. It is important that these companies are approached before the new employee joins. Of course, it has to be done with the permission of the person concerned. Many companies do not contact an interviewee's present employers until the job has been offered ('subject to references'). It is foolish not to do it at all, though.

Activity 25

2 mins

Why do you think it is important to check up on references?

_____

_____

_____

It is important to verify that:

■ the candidate has had the experience claimed;
■ they have a good record of timekeeping, honesty and so on.

It's as well to bear in mind when you are reading references that most people are reluctant to write anything too damning about a former or current employee. It is often more important to take note of what has not been said. For instance, a reference may say that someone is 'willing, pleasant and well-liked' but say very little about competence in the job. Beware of unscrupulous employers who give a glowing reference for somebody they wish to move on.

Activity 26

3 mins

Assume you receive a reference which includes the following statements. Think about what might not be being said. What less virtuous meaning might lie behind each one?

'She's very good at following instructions.'

_____

'She's a good team worker.'

_____

'She gets through her work very quickly'.

_____

You might consider the possibility that

■ someone who is good at following instructions may not be very self-motivated;

■ someone who is a good team worker may get along very well socially or may rely on other members of the team to carry her;

■ someone who gets through work very quickly may be impatient or careless.

Of course there are not always hidden meanings, and it is important not to be overly suspicious, but it is as well to combine the knowledge of the person you gain from an interview with what other people say – and try to read between the lines.

If you are at all uncertain about a reference, you can always telephone the referee. People are often more willing to give an unguarded response on the telephone than they are to write down what they really think.

The next thing you have to do is to make arrangements for the selected candidate to be sent a formal letter offering the job. Once the chosen candidate has accepted, and a start date has been agreed, unsuccessful interviewees should then be sent a letter informing them of the fact.

Activity 27

2 mins

Would you notify the unsuccessful candidates at the same time as the successful ones? Explain your answer.

_____

_____

You have probably said that it is sensible to keep one or two 'runners up' in reserve, in case the first person offered the job doesn't accept.

It is important not to forget the people you've interviewed. Too many companies neglect to notify the ones who don't get the job within a reasonable time period.

The next step is to look back and learn. It is important to ask yourself the following questions, especially if this was your first experience of interviewing.

What did you learn from the interviews?

- Did they go as planned?
- What would you do differently next time?
- Learn as much as you can from the experience.

| Portfolio of evidence C7.2 | Activity 28 | 30 mins |

This Activity may provide the basis of appropriate evidence for your S/NVQ portfolio. If you are intending to take this course of action, it might be better to write your answers on separate sheets of paper.

1 Make contact with whoever has responsibility for advertising posts. When a vacancy occurs ask for a chance to work with those responsible to draft an advert for the relevant press. Keep notes of what factors you considered in deciding what to put in the advert and where to advertise.

2 Try and gain an opportunity to get involved in shortlisting candidates for interview. Keep notes about:
   - how you compared the application forms against the job description and person specification for the post;
   - what influenced your judgement about the candidates at this point in the selection process;
   - which candidates you shortlisted and why.

3 You may be able to participate in the interview, ideally from start to finish. Keep notes on:
   - how you felt during the interview;
   - what questions you asked and why;
   - how they helped you identify the right candidate for the job.

   Ask for feedback from others in the interview process about your questioning technique. Compose letters inviting the candidates to interview and following up the interview. Keep copies as evidence.

4 Find out your organization's policy on considering internal candidates and why. Consider whether you would like to make greater use of internal candidates in the future.

   Include the report of your findings and considerations in your portfolio.

Self-assessment 2

15 mins

1   A good interviewer spends most of the time listening, because:

   a   listening is the best way to learn;
   b   listening is more professional than talking;
   c   listening encourages the interviewee to divulge information;
   d   most candidates talk themselves into, or out of, a job.

2   Which of the following statements is correct?

   Notes are essential because:

   a   they remind the interviewer of what was said, and what observations were made;
   b   they help when comparing candidates;
   c   they give the interviewer something to do during the pauses;
   d   they give a candidate a good idea of how well things went.

3   Fill in the missing words from the list below.

   facts   failures   main   purpose   specified   experience

   The _____ of a job selection interview is to determine the

   _____ about a candidate in terms of knowledge, _____,

   past achievements and _____ , in order to ascertain whether they

   are likely to do a _____ job well.

4   Which of the following questions can be described as open questions?

   a   'Tell me about your last job?'
   b   'Where do you live?'
   c   'Can you describe to me how you first came into marketing?'
   d   'How many children have you?'

5   Which of the following is **not** a key step to achieving success in an interview?

   a   plan and prepare
   b   listen
   c   summarize
   d   ask plenty of closed questions
   e   look back and learn

   Fill in the blanks in the following sentences with a suitable word.

6   Open questions give the interviewee the _____ to _____ freely.

7   The task of the interviewer is to prompt, _____ and _____.

8 Which of the following statements about references is true?

a References often contain lies about candidates.
b References can provide confirmation of a candidate's statements.
c References provide a record of a candidate's timekeeping and honesty.
d References are better given over the phone.

Answers to these questions can be found on pages 74–5.

13 Summary

- The main functions of an interviewer are to:
  - put candidates at their ease;
  - prompt candidates into talking about themselves and their experience;
  - listen.

- Interview preparation involves:
  - preparing a list of appropriate candidates;
  - making use of the job description and person specification;
  - organizing a suitable place to hold the interview.

- The interview has several stages:
  - opening remarks;
  - the job and the organization;
  - direct questions about facts on the application form;
  - open questions about the background, experience and ability of the candidate;
  - interviewee asking questions;
  - summary and the next step;
  - tour of the workplace.

- A good interviewer:
  - remembers to listen;
  - shows interest;
  - aims to keep the interviewee relaxed;
  - avoids conflict.

- When assessing applications:
  - use the job specification as a checklist;
  - ignore job titles;
  - look at past performance;
  - devise an appropriate ranking or scoring system to help you compare candidates.

- When following up interviews, make sure you:
  - check up on references;
  - notify the successful candidate;
  - notify the unsuccessful candidates;
  - look back and learn.

Session C Helping the new employee

... I've got a new one-dimensional measure of excellence.
Would you want your son or daughter to work there?
What would such a place be, in order to be good enough for your kids?
Ethical? Profitable? Growing? Yes. Yes. Yes.
Also, if you ask me, spirited, spunky. And curious. And a place where they're routinely told, 'Do something great!'
Maybe the list for your kids is different. Somehow I bet it isn't, or not much.

Tom Peters, *Crazy Times Call for Crazy Organizations*

1 Introduction

EXTENSION 3
You will find it useful to read about induction in *Supervisory Management* by D. Evans.

Introducing a new member of staff to your team is an important and time-consuming task for the line manager, requiring a lot of thought and planning. Contrary to popular belief – and common practice – it does not simply consist of a chat on the first day with new recruits, thereafter leaving them to their own devices.

In this session you will be looking at exactly what a proper induction process should involve – possibly more than you thought!

2 Preparing for the new employee

The interviewing is over. You've selected the person you want and the starting date has been agreed. What now? Let's first think about some matters of administration. You may have to check:

- whether a written contract of employment has to be drawn up and, if so, by whom;
- whether a medical examination will have to be arranged;
- who will arrange to give the new starter the statement of terms and conditions of service which must be given to a new employee within thirteen weeks of starting.

Do you have to do any of these things, or make a contribution? Always check this with HRD or with your manager, so that there is a smooth transition from making the appointment to the new member taking up the post.

39

You won't want to be as unprepared as the line manager in our next case study was.

■ I had advertised for a new sales manager and was very pleased with the one we found. It was the summer and I was away on holiday for the two weeks before his starting date. Before going away I had made some preparations for his arrival and had briefly talked about it with my PA, but as there were lots of other things to do I didn't run through things as thoroughly as I should have.

He arrived in the office that morning about twenty minutes after I got there. Lots of problems had cropped up while I had been away, and I was trying to sort some of them out. So I just hadn't given him a thought when he was announced and brought in. He can't have been very impressed. I tried to carry out a normal induction session with him that day, but my mind was elsewhere – I was trying to work out solutions to the problems that had arisen, and I was constantly interrupted by calls and other members of staff. I didn't have any of the paperwork ready. I had to spend a lot of time tracking it down.

I know now that I need to give myself at least a day in the office before a new person starts, to get all the papers ready and think over what I need to say.

The lack of thought and preparation this story illustrates isn't that unusual. To say that this is rather unfair on the new starter is to state the obvious. Less obvious is the fact that it is against the supervisor's interests.

Activity 29

3 mins

Imagine a new recruit will be starting work in your section in a week. What are the main things you hope to achieve in the new recruit's first few weeks in the workplace and how would you go about achieving them?

_____

_____

_____

_____

_____

_____

You may have answered:

■ to make the new person's introduction as smooth as possible;
■ to give a good impression of the company;
■ to make the new recruit an effective member of the team as soon as possible.

Depending on what the job is, you may need to:

'People ask for criticism, but they only want praise.'

W. Somerset Maugham, *Of Human Bondage* (1915) ch. 50

- prepare a working space for the new person;
- plan what you want them to learn;
- decide who they will work with;
- obtain any equipment or materials that will be needed;
- make sure that any security arrangements are made, such as passes, clearance to enter buildings, etc.;
- set up a timetable or programme of induction and training, so that there are no hitches in getting the starter up to full working efficiency.

Above all, as a line manager, it is in your interest to:

- provide a warm welcome to new members of staff;
- put them at their ease;
- be patient during the initial period and give the starter time to settle down.

3 Introduction to the organization

A new member of staff is probably totally in the dark about how your team or the organization as a whole works. Nothing is obvious until it is pointed out to you.

Activity 30

20 mins

'When you go to work tomorrow, try to look at "your place" as a fearful, first day employee would.'

Tom Peters, *Crazy Times Call for Crazy Organizations*

Think back to a recent occasion when you appointed a new person to your area or department. What information did you pass on to them when they first started? What information did the HRD give to them as well? How was the information given? Assemble any written material (plus videos and cassettes if applicable) and make a summary of what information was covered. If you haven't recently appointed anyone, work out now what information you would give a new recruit and in what format and, if appropriate, what information your HRD would give them.

_____

_____

_____

_____

_____

_____

_____

_____

Here is a comprehensive list of the information you could give a new recruit.

3.1 General information

- An explanation of the structure of the organization, with special reference to the particular section where the newcomer will work. Your name and the name of your manager.
- A brief account of the organization's history and ownership.
- The products or services produced, and the benefits they bring to users.
- What social and sports activities and arrangements are available.
- Which trade unions are recognized and how to contact their representatives.
- A confirmation of the new employee's job title and status, and in broad terms what the job entails.

3.2 Information about the rules

- All the terms and conditions of employment, including a confirmation of the starting salary or wage and rules about probationary periods.
- General rules to be obeyed, such as:

  - signing-in or clocking-on procedures;
  - rules about lateness, absenteeism and so on;
  - what the hours of work are, and any shift arrangements;
  - where and when smoking is allowed;
  - any mandatory safety rules applying to the whole area.

- The salaries and payments conditions: procedures for sickness absence and benefit, payments for overtime and shift work, any payments for special conditions and holiday payments.

3.3 Health and safety information

- Emergency procedures.
- Hazardous areas.
- The location of first aid and medical centres, and refuge areas.
- Protective clothing, and how to use it.

Remember that the newcomer will almost certainly have difficulty in taking everything in, so provide the information using more than one medium:

- by word of mouth;
- using printed materials;
- handwritten notes;
- other methods such as videos and audio tapes.

Activity 31

10 mins

Are the procedures for health and safety induction in your place of work well documented? If not, what can you do to help get them formalized? Make a note here of any action you could take in this respect.

_____

_____

_____

_____

Newcomers will want to meet the colleagues they are to work with, and to become familiar with the area. They should have a conducted tour of the work area, and in large workplaces a map would be useful.

4 Introduction to the job

Now down to work. What is the most effective way of getting a newcomer started on the job?

Activity 32

4 mins

One of the most common ways of training people for a job is to put them alongside an experienced worker, to learn largely by observation and imitation. Jot down the advantages and disadvantage of this method.

_____

_____

_____

_____

This method has its advantages as it is not expensive, and it doesn't take up much of the line manager's time. But the disadvantages can outweigh the advantages:

- the learner will pick up all the bad habits of the skilled worker, as well as the good ones;
- there is often little incentive for the 'teacher' to be helpful; they may feel rather resentful about having to give up their time to the newcomer;
- the learner is less likely to be told the reasons for doing things in a certain way.

43

Activity 33

4 mins

Now think of this question in terms of your own job. What would be the best way to be introduced to it?

_____

_____

_____

_____

Your answer will depend on the job you and your team do, but everyone should ideally have the opportunity to:

- go through a planned formal training programme, appropriate to the job;
- learn from someone skilled at teaching or instructing, with the time to give full attention to the new recruit;
- learn the theory or the reasons behind the procedures and approach to the job: even in the most routine task.

5 Individual needs

So far we have looked very generally at the best way of helping a new person feel comfortable in a new setting. Some people will require more help in certain respects.

5.1 School leavers

School leavers deserve special mention as they are unlikely to have had much first-hand experience of working life and often find it difficult to settle down.

Activity 34

3 mins

What are the main differences between school and work which may explain this problem? Try to list three.

_____

_____

_____

Some of the main differences include:

- longer hours;
- less variety in the work done;
- work which may involve using the hands and 'thinking on one's feet', rather than sitting at a desk;
- health and safety hazards;
- being surrounded by adults.

Activity 35

3 mins

What could you do to reduce the culture shock that a school leaver may suffer?

_____

_____

_____

You could:

- explain safety and other rules more carefully and be sympathetic when answering any naive questions;
- try to give varied and interesting jobs, so that the youngster can have a chance to develop a range of skills;
- discourage any attempt by other team members to take advantage of the school leaver's immaturity or junior status.

5.2 People with disabilities

EXTENSION 4
You can find out more about the legal provision for people with various disabilities in The Disability Discrimination Act 1995.

The Disability Discrimination Act 1995 states that a person is disabled if he or she has:

'a physical or mental impairment which has a substantial and long-term adverse effect on his or her ability to carry out normal, day-to-day activities'.

The most common reasons why people with disabilities find it difficult to find jobs or to keep them has more to do with the attitude of employers than with their disabilities. In turn, employers generally reflect the attitude of society. If someone is in a wheelchair or has some other disability, then it is often assumed that he or she will be less efficient and will require special facilities that are costly to provide.

Activity 36

2 mins

What is your feeling about employing – or working – with people with disabilities? Think back to any experience you have had of employing or working with people with disabilities. Comment on this experience.

_____

_____

_____

_____

EXTENSION 5
The Code of Good Practice on the Employment of Disabled People, which is promoted by the Department for Education and Employment, contains a clear, practical guide which outlines a sensible approach to employing disabled people.

It is as well to be aware of your own attitude towards working with people who may seem in some way 'different', to learn whether there are practical steps which can be taken to ease the situation, or whether any problems may be to do with your own – or your colleagues' attitude.

The Code of Good Practice on the Employment of Disabled People makes these important points:

- Most disabled people have the same skills and abilities to offer as able-bodied people and are effective as employees without the need for any special help.
- Many other disabled people have as much to offer as able-bodied people, given the use of appropriate help which is readily available.
- When the abilities of disabled workers are overlooked, companies are missing out on a contribution of potentially valuable employees.
- Employers have obligations, along with the rest of society, to ensure that disabled people are treated fairly.

Activity 37

4 mins

How well is the place where you work geared up for people with disabilities? What improvements could be made to existing arrangements?

_____

_____

_____

_____

_____

_____

Clearly we can't answer the first question, but it is important to give some thought to this issue. It may be necessary to install ramps or lifts for wheelchair users or people who have difficulty walking; a loop system can be of benefit to many (but not all) people with hearing loss. Refer to *The Code of Good Practice on the Employment of Disabled People* for other practical suggestions.

5.3 Part-timers and job sharers

Changes in work patterns and demographic trends over the last few years have meant greater flexibility in the ways in which people work.

Activity 38

4 mins

What problems or special needs can you foresee for people who are not working full-time within your organization?

_____

_____

_____

_____

It's likely to take people longer to become accustomed to a new organization, its culture and ways of doing things. It is well known that people who are actually sharing a job, and expected to work two and a half days per week, often work far more than their allocated time. Resentments can build up over time and people may feel that they are being taken advantage of, so it is as well to make your position clear and reassure both job sharers that you have no intention of exploiting them. It is also important to recognize that there may be some rivalry – as well as different ways of working – between the two people concerned. It is wise to play on their strengths rather than trying to find their weaknesses – this way you will certainly benefit from having the skills and knowledge of two people.

Self-assessment 3

20 mins

Complete the sentences below using these words.

exploitation   familiarization   boredom
induction   training

1   The process of _____ is the formal introduction to an organization

    and involves _____ and _____.

2   School leavers must be protected from _____ and _____.

    Answer the following questions:

3   List two objectives which you would aim to achieve during a new starter's
    first weeks on the job.

4   Briefly state three ways of learning a new job.

5   List four things that new employees need information about.

6   List three ways in which you can help a new employee to become effective as
    soon as possible.

7   Suggest two things which can be done to help school leavers adjust more
    quickly to a new job.

8   What is the name of the law which relates to people with disabilities at
    work?

Answers to these questions can be found on page 75.

6 Summary

- Your aim in the induction process is to:

  - help the person become used to the organization and the job as quickly as possible
  - give a good impression of the organization.

- Induction involves providing information about:

  - the organization
  - the rules
  - health and safety
  - the job
  - available facilities
  - the people and the physical environment
  - training.

- You will need to ensure that the new employee has access to:

  - the theory behind the job
  - any formal training which is necessary
  - frequent advice and help.

- It is not appropriate to lay down exactly the same set of induction guidelines for everyone. Those we have identified are school leavers, people with disabilities and part time members of staff.

Session D Keeping your staff

To: Inc magazine

From: Determinedly Seeking the Perfect Job

I don't want to screw around any more in a place that's badly managed, poorly run and so stupid I'm just wasting my time. Or a place where you have to be a vice-president to get a window. I want to take my dogs to work, at least on Saturdays, and if I break into a chorus of 'Oklahoma' at 4 p.m., I want two people to harmonize with me – not look at me sideways.

I want to work cooperatively in a team. I don't care so much what industry it is, but the more socially conscious, the better. I want an environment that's honest, supportive, fair, inclusive, and playful. I'm really great at what I do, and now I'm going to find a really great place to do it in. I want flexi time and exercise space and community service and lots of chances to learn. I want trees and easy parking!

Signed, Determined

Tom Peters, *Crazy Times Call for Crazy Organizations*

1 Introduction

All the effort, resources and money put into finding new employees is wasted if they don't stay in their jobs long. In this session we will look at some of the reasons why staff stay in a job and the systems and skills that could be in place to ensure that you know how your staff are coping.

2 Reasons for staying

People stay in a job or a particular organization for any number of reasons, some of them practical such as:

- because the job is located conveniently, and
- the working hours suit their other commitments.

Some reasons are more emotive, such as:

- they get on well with their work mates
- they enjoy what they do.

51

Activity 39

Consider your own working life. Think about the things that make you happy and things that have made you unhappy and may have made you think of looking for another job. Also think of comments that you might have heard from work colleagues about how contented or discontented they are. Now write a list of all the characteristics of a place of work that would encourage you and other people to stay in a job.

_____

_____

_____

_____

_____

Your list might include:

- I enjoyed going to work there, as people were friendly and helpful;
- It was hard work, but I felt rewarded because everyone appreciated my contribution;
- The pay was fair and the work was interesting;
- I was part of a team and we all pulled together;
- Although my job was a very small part of the work of the company I was never made to feel small;
- I always knew where I stood, my manager was always fair with me and often told me what I was good at, as well as where I needed to do better;
- Staff were often asked for ideas and consulted on any big changes that would affect the way we worked;
- There was the opportunity for further training if we were expected to do things in a different way.

You'll see from this list that although getting the right pay for the job is mentioned, and is always important, it is equally important for staff to:

- feel valued and appreciated
- know where they stand
- get fair and honest feedback about their performance
- have the right skills for the job
- be involved in changes.

3 Feeling valued

It is a basic human need for us to feel valued or appreciated by our friends, family and work colleagues. This applies at whatever level in the organization we are working.

It is important to remember that the major part of any organization are the people that work there. If an organization invests in and respects its workforce then it will work more effectively and efficiently. This is a person-centred approach to management and is gaining in popularity. An interesting case is where a consultant, using a person-centred approach, was allowed by a large industrial firm to perform an experiment. In the experimental plants, where the person-centred approach was used, the average cost of a particular unit was 22 cents. In the non-experimental plants the same item cost 70 cents. The firm prevented the consultant from publicizing his work because the profit gain was so large it was regarded as confidential. How ironic that treating people as people should be regarded as a trade secret!

Activity 40

3 mins

Try to describe the term 'person-centred approach'. Comment on how it applies to your organization.

_____

_____

_____

_____

_____

'The art of being wise is the art of knowing what to overlook.'

William James, *The Principles of Psychology* (1890), ch. 22

The person-centred approach is based on recognizing and acknowledging the value of the individual. People are respected, cared for and listened to. There is an attempt to meet their needs and to place them at the centre and base of the organization.

4 Giving and receiving feedback

We all like to know how we're doing and how others see us. However, many people's experience of receiving either feedback or criticism is negative or even humiliating. We probably all find it easier to tell someone how wonderful they are, but what about when we need to let them know there is room for improvement? Giving feedback can be a good experience, if done constructively.

What's the difference between feedback and criticism? When given well, both offer the information about the effect of a person's behaviour or performance. Both can start a process that leads to development and change. Both work best where the relationship between the giver and the receiver is already open, honest and respectful.

Remember that feedback:

■ is offered for the receiver's benefit;
■ leaves the receiver free to decide what to do with the information they receive;
■ implies an equal relationship and can be distorted by hierarchy;
■ is not judgmental;
■ works best with 'I' statements such as 'I thought you spoke rather slowly'.

Criticism, on the other hand:

■ is given because the giver wants a change or improvement;
■ usually asks or demands that the other person changes;
■ often arises within a hierarchy (the person in charge wants a change in behaviour);
■ is judgmental;
■ often includes 'you' statements, for example, 'you speak too slowly'.

To give constructive feedback or criticism well, it helps if you:

■ plan ahead – decide exactly what you want to say, avoiding snap judgements or comments about things that cannot be changed;
■ practice observing what goes well as much as what could be improved;
■ consider the time and place before you begin – ample time and privacy are important;
■ say specifically what you observe and think is going well – this can form a positive foundation on which to build improvements. However, most people find positive information hard to accept at first. So be specific and give details and examples;
■ aim to give twice as much positive information as negative. It may help to write down the positive information.
■ be equally specific about what you think could or should be improved. Select what you say and avoid nit picking. Respect the person you are talking to. It is only appropriate to comment on what the person does, not who the person is;

'If we had no
faults of our own,
we would not take
so much pleasure
in noticing those
of others.'

Francis, Duc de La
Rochefoucauld
*Reflections; or,
Sentences and
Moral Maxims*
(1678), Maxim 31

- give facts, not opinions;
- if you are giving constructive criticism, say what changes you expect and assist the person to work out how they will achieve these. You may also set a time for review.

Giving feedback and constructive criticism should be an ongoing activity. Staff should always be clear about how colleagues and line managers feel about their work. Your staff will gain much more if you are open and honest and encourage feedback amongst and between colleagues. Your organization may have formalized this feedback process on a regular basis through some type of appraisal scheme.

Activity 41

3 mins

Think back over the last week at work. Make a list of how often you have received or given feedback or constructive criticism from and to work colleagues. Was there any time in the week where you would have found it helpful or motivating to receive more positive feedback on something you had done?

_____

_____

_____

Now think of feedback you have received, either negative or positive. What effect did it have?

_____

_____

_____

It is quite likely that you have received no feedback at all. Many people go for weeks without any comment on their work, so they really have no idea whether they are doing well or badly. This can only contribute to a feeling of routineness – if there is no appreciation and no attempt to acknowledge difficulties either, it is almost impossible for people to improve and quite difficult even to take pride in work.

Constructive criticism, if thoughtfully given, is usually helpful in pointing out ways in which the job could have been done better/more quickly/or more in line with the organization's demands. Praise can be even more valuable, in giving people a glow of satisfaction which makes all their hard work worthwhile. Thoughtless or harsh criticism, on the other hand, can be very damaging; many people will respond by doing even less work, or taking less care.

It is worth thinking carefully about what you say to people and considering the possible effects of the words you use.

5 Developing staff

Most people hope to develop and grow in their jobs. Organizations offering opportunities for training and development are likely to keep their staff longer and get more from them.

... a casual approach to continued learning will not do. Secretaries and receptionists, along with software engineers and lending officers, are already competing directly in the global labour market, and that competitive pressure will only intensify (by order of magnitude) in the years to come. The way you win ... is to acquire new skills constantly.

Tom Peters, *Crazy Times for Crazy Organizations*

Activity 42   3 mins

Tom Peters suggests asking yourself:

Just what have you learned in the last three months?

_____

six months?

_____

one year?

_____

18 months?

_____

And now prove it.

_____

_____

_____

56

If you could not think of anything, now is the time to ask yourself some questions about your approach to your job, such as:

- What new skills do I want to learn this year?
- What old skills can I update or enhance?
- How can I be more valuable to the organization?
- What is your strategic plan for the next three years?

And of course, ask these same questions of your team members.

On the other hand, it is quite possible that you have learned something which has nothing, on the face of it, to do with work, but which may nevertheless have some impact on the job you do. For example, involvement in a local drama group may have taught you a great deal about working in teams and the need for everyone to pull together to achieve a common goal.

One of your roles should be to make ongoing assessments (or appraisals) of staff's present performance together with an attempt to match this against future needs. If you have taken the task of giving feedback seriously, you may have identifed some gaps in people's performance which could be filled by training. The sorts of questions you should be asking about all members of your team are:

- Is he or she up to the job technically?
- Is he or she ready for promotion?
- Can he or she be left to get on with the job without being supervised all the time?

Everyone in your team should have a development plan, with specific goals. You will need to decide now about the potential for the future, even if the future is only tomorrow. Talking to your team members and asking them how **they** would like to develop and in which directions, should help you to formulate training plans.

Portfolio of evidence C7.1

Activity 43

30 mins

This Activity may provide the basis of appropriate evidence for your S/NVQ portfolio. If you are intending to take this course of action, it might be better to write your answers on separate sheets of paper.

1   Draw up an outline development plan for your team. (Your plan may incorporate the need for new staff.) Take into account the needs and aims of individual members of your team as well as those of the organization. Keep notes or write **brief** reports of discussions or meetings you have with your workteam members and with management.

Be sure to take into account any organizational policy (including mission statement and objectives) as well as legal requirements for all members of your team.

2   Present your plan in the form of a report to your manager.

Self-assessment 4

20 mins

Complete the following sentences with an appropriate word.

1 It is a basic human need for us to feel _____ by our work colleagues.

2 Treating employees with mutual respect, in an open and honest way and valuing their opinions is sometimes called the _____ centred approach to management.

3 In giving feedback and/or constructive criticism you should aim to give _____ as much _____ information as _____ information.

4 Which two of the following statements describes feedback:

   a it is not judgmental

   b it often includes 'you' statements

   c it implies an equal relationship

   d it demands the person changes

5 Why is staff development an important aspect of keeping staff?

   _____

6 List three questions you should ask about yourself and your staff to demonstrate that you are really concerned with growth and development.

   _____

   _____

   _____

Answers to these questions can be found on page 76.

6 Summary

- People are likely to stay longer in a job if they:

  - feel valued and appreciated;
  - know where they stand;
  - get fair and honest feedback about their performance;
  - have the right skills for the job;
  - are involved in changes.

- It is important to know how to give feedback and constructive criticism. They should be given regularly and should be specific and based on facts.

- Most people want to grow and develop in their jobs. You need to be asking questions about:

  - what people could do better;
  - what they want to learn;
  - and how they can be more valuable to the organization.

- You are more likely to keep good staff if you:

  - identify training needs;
  - match individual aspirations with the needs of the organization;
  - help people to enhance their skills.

Performance checks

In the space below, write down your answer to the following questions on *Securing the Right People*.

Question 1   What and who must you consider when a post becomes vacant?

_____

_____

_____

Question 2   When starting to analyse a job, what questions should you be asking?

_____

_____

_____

Question 3   What is the difference between a job description and a person specification?

_____

_____

Question 4   What are the most usual methods of attracting applicants to jobs?

_____

_____

Question 5   Which three laws are particularly relevant to recruitment?

_____

_____

Question 6   What are the main functions of an interviewer?

_____

_____

_____

_____

Question 7   Why is it so important to take notes in an interview?

_____

_____

Question 8   Briefly describe the scoring method of assessing candidates.

_____

_____

_____

Question 9   List three pitfalls of the scoring assessment.

_____

_____

_____

Question 10   What benefits can be gained by the organization if new staff are given an induction programme?

_____

_____

_____

Question 11   List five items that you would include on an induction programme checklist.

_____

_____

_____

_____

_____

Question 12   Explain the individual needs of a new employee with a disability.

_____

_____

_____

_____

Question 13   What will you specifically need to take into account when planning an induction programme for a school leaver?

_____

_____

_____

_____

Question 14 How would you define a person centred approach to management?

_____

_____

_____

Question 15 Why is it important to retain staff, as well as be good at recruiting them?

_____

_____

_____

Answers to these questions can be found on pages 75–7.

2 Workbook assessment

60
mins

Read the following case incident and then answer the questions that follow. You should write the answer to the questions on a separate sheet of paper.

■ Aquarius is a medium sized company that supplies component parts for the motor racing industry. There are 300 people employed and they are based in two sites about two miles apart.

The majority of the staff are used to working in small teams of 4–6 and they share responsibility for ensuring the quality of their work and ensuring the jobs get done to agreed targets.

The stock control department is based on one of the sites, but holds the stock of parts for both sites. The stock control team consists of a stock control manager (David), three part-time stock control clerks, a junior (Paul) and senior store person (George) and a part-time van delivery driver (Joyce). The driver delivers components between the sites and to local customers. The staff in the department are well known to most of the company's employees, because they supply the teams with the raw materials to do their jobs.

Paul, the junior store person, has decided he would like to go to college full time to get a qualification to help him get a job in the leisure industry. He had taken this job straight from school not knowing what he really wanted to do long term. The stock control manager had hoped he could train him up to take on George's job when he retires in 18 months time.

Paul is required to give two weeks' notice to the company, and he does this in writing after a conversation with David about his intentions. When the team hears of Paul's intention to leave, Joyce asks David if she can increase her hours and combine Paul's job with her own. George comes to see David in a panic saying he can't possibly manage without someone to replace Paul immediately.

On the same day as hearing the news and having the representations from the staff, David is called to a heads of team meeting where they are all asked to see how they could make staff savings of 5%.

1   Paul handing in his notice creates a vacancy in David's team. List the steps David should take, and why, before automatically advertising the vacancy.

2   Why is shortlisting part of the selection process and what does David need to consider when shortlisting any applicants for the job?

3   List all the things David will need to consider during and when preparing for the interviews. Write a paragraph explaining everything on your list, why it is important and anything you know about what constitutes good interviewing practice.

4   The new applicant is appointed and starts next week. What should David take into account when organizing an induction programme for the new person?

5   Why do you think it might be important for David to interview Paul before he leaves? What could be gained by conducting a termination or exit interview?

| Portfolio of evidence C7.1, C7.2 | **3 Work-based assignment** | 60 mins |

The time guide for this assignment gives you an approximate idea of how long it is likely to take you to write up your findings. You will need to spend some additional time gathering information, perhaps talking to colleagues or thinking about your assignment.

Your written response to this assignment may provide the basis of appropriate evidence for your S/NVQ portfolio.

What you have to do

For this assignment, your aim is to carry out an evaluation of the recruitment process in your organization.

1   You will need, first of all, to find out exactly who is involved, and to what extent, in the process. Talking to these people will give you a clearer picture of the different parts of the process, so that you can begin to piece together the whole picture. (You may find it helpful to think about the process you went through when you were recruited – particularly if this wasn't too long ago.)

Then you will need to analyse the process. Try to evaluate each step of the way, **how** it works and **why** it works well or badly. Once again, it will be helpful to talk to people, other employees and perhaps people who were unsuccessful in their interviews.

2   Remember that an important part of the recruitment process is keeping people who are valuable to the organization. What steps are taken to do this? How successful are they? What could be done better? Ask your team members why they remain working for the organization. What useful ideas could be taken forward to improve induction or staff development?

What you should write

Prepare a report for your manager based on your discussions with your colleagues at all levels. Try to convey the overall aim and approach of the organization's recruiting policies as well as highlighting particularly important stages or ideas.

Your report should cover both the recruiting aspects and also the retention aspects of this larger process. Identify things which could be improved and put forward recommendations for change.

Your report does not need to be long – two or three pages. But it must convey a clear understanding of what goes on in the organization and convince the reader that you have thought carefully about possible areas for improvement.

Reflect and review

Now that you have completed your work on *Securing the Right People*, let us review our workbook objectives.

■   When you have completed this workbook, you will be better able to take part in the recruitment and selection process.

In this workbook we have stressed the importance of finding the 'right' people – people who are right for the job and right for the organization. This process involves making a close match between the needs of the organization and the skills, knowledge and experience of the successful candidate or, in other words, fitting a round peg into a round hole.

Now that you have completed your reading and responded to the Activities, you will perhaps have a better understanding of the recruitment process and its part in the overall personnel function. You should also be much more aware of the part you have to play in this important aspect of the management of the organization.

Try the following questions.

■ Why is it important for first line managers to be a part of the recruitment and selection process, rather than just leaving it all to the personnel department? What can you do to make sure you play as active and effective a role as possible in this process?

_____

_____

_____

_____

_____

_____

_____

67

■ How does the recruitment process work in your organization? What could you do to make sure it works as smoothly as possible?

_____

_____

_____

_____

_____

_____

_____

_____

The second objective was:

■ You will be better able to prepare for interviews.

The choice of new staff is notoriously difficult. Traditionally an interview is the method adopted by most organizations to try to find out whether a candidate is suitable for the post in question. It is not possible simply to walk into the interview room and ask lots of questions – there are important preparations to be made if the best use is to be made of this time – which can be nerve racking for the people on both sides of the desk!

■ Why do you think interviewing is such a common way of selecting new staff?

_____

_____

_____

_____

■ What preparations do you currently make for interviews? As a result of what you've learned, how will you do things differently now?

_____

_____

_____

_____

_____

_____

_____

_____

_____

The third objective was:

■ You will be better able to plan, prepare and carry out an effective interview.

Having looked at the overall process of recruitment, we looked at the main way of evaluating candidates: the interview. The role of the interviewer is a key one and we stressed the importance of listening to candidates in order to find out as much as possible about their experience and achievements. Good interviewers can match candidates to jobs, recognizing who will fit where and who will be able to make a contribution to the organization.

It takes time to develop interview skills – for either side of the table! From your vantage point, the aim is to facilitate the communication process so that you select the best person for the job.

■ As an interviewer, what do you see as your main roles?

_____

_____

■ What techniques do you use to get interviewees to talk about themselves?

_____

_____

The fourth objective was:

■ You will be better able to assess the information you obtain during an interview.

It is all too easy to gain a great deal of information from interviews – and then to forget it, or be unable to use it to make the right choice. The interview is worthless unless you have some way of evaluating the information you gain. There are a number of methods for organizing this information and helping you to make an informed choice.

■ What system do you use for assessing candidates? Do you think this is the most appropriate method? If you don't already have a system, describe how you would assess candidates in the future.

_____

_____

_____

_____

_____

_____

69

■ What can you do to avoid some of the pitfalls of assessment?

_____

_____

_____

_____

_____

_____

The fifth objective was:

■ You will be better able to plan and implement good induction schemes for your workteam.

The process of recruitment doesn't stop with hiring the successful candidate. It is to everyone's advantage to ensure that the new team member settles into the job and the organization as soon as possible. Induction facilitates this process.

We have suggested that you try to look at your organization (or at least your work section) through the eyes of a new employee – what do you see? What is likely to help you settle in and learn your job quickly? How could you be made more welcome or encouraged to feel more confident about your work and your position within the organization?

■ How would you assess the induction programme you provide for new staff with what you have learnt to be good practice in the unit? How could things be improved and what aspects of the current approach would you keep?

_____

_____

_____

■ Taking account of your team situation and using the principles of induction, what would you include in an ideal programme for the next member of staff to join your team?

_____

_____

_____

The sixth objective was:

■ You will be better able to design and implement policies related to staff retention.

Once new staff have been satisfactorily inducted, there has already been a considerable investment in time and money. It is in everyone's best interests that staff remain with the organization and make the best contribution that they can. A knowledge of what individual staff want from their work as well as an overview of the aims of the organization will be invaluable in helping you to develop staff to reach their greatest potential. And if and when staff do eventually leave, don't forget to include them in this end of the recruitment process – to find out why they are going so that you can refine the initial stages of the recruitment process to take account of their experiences.

■ What conditions need to be present in an organization to get the best from staff and encourage them to stay? How does your organization compare with the list you have made?

_____

_____

_____

_____

■ Is there any part of the recruitment and selection process which is more important than another in helping to retain staff in an organization?

_____

_____

_____

_____

2 Action plan

Use this plan to further develop for yourself a course of action you want to take. Make a note in the left-hand column of the issues or problems you want to tackle, and then decide what you intend to do, and make a note in Column 2.

The resources you need might include time, materials, information or money. You may need to negotiate for some of them, but they could be something easily acquired, like half an hour of somebody's time, or a chapter of a book. Put whatever you need in Column 3. No plan means anything without a timescale, so put a realistic target completion date in Column 4.

Finally, describe the outcome you want to achieve as a result of this plan, whether it is for your own benefit or advancement, or a more efficient way of doing things.

Desired outcomes				Actual outcomes
1 Issues	2 Action	3 Resources	4 Target completion	

3 Extensions

Extension 1

Book   *Effective Interviewing*
Author   C. Goodworth
Publisher   Better Business (Hutchinson)

Extension 2

Book   *Management by Effective Listening*
Author   K. J. Murphy
Publisher   Sidgwick and Jackson

Extension 3

Book   *Supervisory Management*
Author   D. Evans
Publisher   Cassells

Extension 4

Book   *The Disability Discrimination Act, 1995*
Publisher   Manpower Services Commission

Extension 5

Book   *The Code of Good Practice on the Employment of Disabled People*

These extensions can be taken up via your NEBS Mangement Centre. They will either have them or will arrange that you have access to them. However, it may be more convenient to check out the materials with your personnel or training people at work – they may well give you access. There are other good reasons for approaching your own people: for example, they will become aware of your interest and you can involve them in your development.

4 Answers to self-assessment questions

Self-assessment 1 on page 15

1 a The first step in the process of filling a vacancy is to find out about your organization's **policies** and **procedures**.
   b A **job description** sets out the responsibilities and tasks of an employee.
   c A job specification consists of a job description and a **person specification**.
   d In cases of dispute, a job description can be a useful **reference document**.

2   You might use the following headings in a person specification:

■ Education and training
■ Qualifications
■ Experience
■ Personal qualities

3   When beginning to draw up a job description you should ask yourself the following questions:

■ What is the job?
■ How will it be done?
■ Where will it be done?
■ When will it be done?
■ Who will do it?

4   Before advertising for new employees, it is essential for you to obtain authorization.

5   To attract the right kind of people to apply, a job advertisement should include brief details of:

■ main duties
■ location
■ wages or salary
■ other incentives
■ hours of work

6   The two most relevant pieces of legislation are the Race Relations Act and the Sex Discrimination Act.

Self-assessment 2 on page 36

1   A good interviewer spends most of the time listening, because (c) an interviewer's task is to prompt the interviewee to divulge information

2   (a) and (b) are correct. Notes are a way of summarizing the facts and impressions of an interview, in order to give the interviewer a better chance of remembering and comparing candidates.

3   The **MAIN PURPOSE** of a job selection interview is to determine the **FACTS** about a candidate in terms of knowledge, **EXPERIENCE**, past achievements and **FAILURES** in order to ascertain whether he or she is likely to do a **SPECIFIED** job well.

4   (a) and (c) are open-ended questions. (b) and (d) allow only limited, straightforward answers.

5   (d) Asking closed questions is unlikely to contribute to a successful interview. They may block a candidate's answers without encouraging him or her to expand on ideas and experiences.

6   Open-ended questions give the interviewee the **OPPORTUNITY** to **TALK** freely.

7   The task of the interviewer is to prompt, **LISTEN** and **LEARN**.

8   (b) References can provide confirmation of a candidate's statements. Although references do not usually lie, they do not always tell the whole truth. Neither do they provide a record of attendance and honesty, though, once again, they can confirm candidates' statements. Sometimes it is possible to have full and frank discussions on the phone about candidates, but this is not always the case, and certainly does not mean that references are better given over the phone.

Self-assessment 3 on page 48

1   The process of **INDUCTION** is the formal introduction to an organization and involves **FAMILIARIZATION** and **TRAINING**.

2   School leavers especially should be protected from **EXPLOITATION** and **BOREDOM**.

3   You should try to

- make the new person's introduction as smooth as possible, and
- give a good impression, for the sake of the company's image.

4   The best ways to learn a new job involve:

- learning from a good instructor
- learning the theory or reasons behind the procedures and approach to the job
- going through a formal training programme

5   New employees need information about:

- the organization
- health and safety
- the rules
- the job.

6   Here are three things which can be done to help new employees become effective team members more quickly:

- prepare a new working space for the person
- make sure that necessary tools and equipment are available
- set up a training or induction timetable.

7   School leavers can be helped by

- being given varied and interesting jobs
- having quite a lot of time with a more experienced colleague
- having a clear explanation of health and safety rules.

8   The Disabilities Discrimination Act 1995

Self-assessment 4 on page 58

1   It is a basic human need for us to feel **VALUED** by our work colleagues.

2   Treating employees with mutual respect, in an open and honest way and valuing their opinions is sometimes called the **PERSON** centred approach to management.

3   In giving feedback and/or constructive criticism you should aim to give **TWICE** as much **POSITIVE** information as **NEGATIVE** information.

4   Feedback is (a) not judgemental and (c) implies an equal relationship.

5   Staff development is important to help people grow and develop in their jobs.

6   You should ask yourself (and your team members):

- What have you learned in the last year?
- What new skills do you want to learn in the next year?
- How can you be more valuable to the organization?

5   Answers to quick quiz

Answer 1   When a post becomes vacant you must consider the implications for the work of your team – how people will feel, as well as how you might be able to use this opportunity to do things differently.

Answer 2   When starting to analyse a job, you should be thinking about the purpose of the job, the performance standards required, the particular contribution this post makes to the overall work of the organization and what would happen if the post wasn't filled.

Answer 3   A job description sets out the responsibilities and tasks of the post and a person specification defines the kind of person who would be most suitable to fill the post.

Answer 4   The most usual methods of attracting applicants to jobs include national and local advertising, advertising in trade magazines and using recruitment agencies.

Answer 5   The three laws which are particularly relevant to recruitment are the Disabilities Discrimination Act, the Sex Discrimination Act and the Race Relations Act.

Answer 6   The main functions of an interviewer are to

- put candidates at their ease
- prompt information from candidates
- listen, to gather information.

Answer 7   Taking notes are an important aid to remembering what candidates have said in the interview. They will also help you to compare candidates and assist the selection process.

Answer 8   The scoring method of assessment involves giving each candidate a score, often out of five, for each of the factors you are considering at the interview, e.g. verbal skills, experience, etc.

Answer 9   Three pitfalls of the scoring method of assessment are:

■ errors of leniency, when candidates are given the benefit of the doubt
■ lack of thought, when not enough attention is paid to the 'fit' between candidate and job
■ the halo effect, when your attitude to one candidate is influenced by your feelings about another, probably previous candidate.

Answer 10   If new staff are given a good induction programme, they will fit in and become more productive members of the workforce more quickly. The organization is more likely to win their long-term loyalty if they have had a good start.

Answer 11   An induction programme checklist should include:

■ information about the organization
■ information about the rules
■ information about health and safety
■ introduction to the area and the people
■ description of the work training programme

Answer 12   A new employee with a disability may need some special adjustments to the physical environment such as stair rails or the provision of a lift or wheel chair access. Mainly they will need patience and an acknowledgement that they are as capable of doing the job they have been hired to do as anyone else – you wouldn't have recruited them otherwise.

Answer 13   When planning an induction programme for a school leaver, you may need to spend a little more time and be a little more patient than usual. It will be important to recognize that a young school leaver is likely to feel even more out of place than an adult. School leavers will benefit from being given interesting and varied jobs and from being given clear explanations of rules and organizational procedures.

Answer 14   The person centred approach to management involves valuing people and acknowledging their skills and experience as well as recognizing that people lie at the heart of the organization and are responsible for its success or failure.

Answer 15   It is important to retain staff as recruiting new staff is an expensive and time-consuming business. Having decided on a candidate who seems to be suitable for the job, it is in everybody's best interests to make sure that he or she is given every opportunity to perform the job to the best of his or her ability.

6 Certificate

Completion of this certificate by an authorized person shows that you have worked through all the parts of this workbook and satisfactorily completed the assessments. The certificate provides a record of what you have done that may be used for exemptions or as evidence of prior learning against other nationally certificated qualifications.

Pergamon Flexible Learning and NEBS Management are always keen to refine and improve their products. One of the key sources of information to help this process are people who have just used the product. If you have any information or views, good or bad, please pass these on.

NEBS
MANAGEMENT
DEVELOPMENT

SUPER SERIES

THIRD EDITION

Securing the Right People

....

has satisfactorily completed this workbook

Name of signatory ....

Position ....

Signature ....

Date ....

Official stamp

SUPER SERIES

To Order - phone us direct for prices and availability details
(please quote ISBNs when ordering)
College orders: 01865 314333 • Account holders: 01865 314301
Individual purchases: 01865 314627 (please have credit card details ready)

We Need Your Views

We really need your views in order to make the Super Series 3 (SS3) an even better learning tool for you. Please take time out to complete and return this questionnaire to Trudi Righton, Pergamon Flexible Learning, Linacre House, Jordan Hill, Oxford, OX2 8DP.

Name : ....

Address : ....

....

Title of workbook : ....

If applicable, please state which qualification you are studying for. If not, please describe what study you are undertaking, and with which organisation or college:

....

Please grade the following out of 10 (10 being extremely good, 0 being extremely poor):

Content   ....   Appropriateness to your position   ....

Readability   ....   Qualification coverage   ....

What did you particularly like about this workbook?

....
....
....

Are there any features you disliked about this workbook? Please identify them.

....
....
....

Are there any errors we have missed? If so, please state page number: ....

How are you using the material? For example, as an open learning course, as a reference resource, as a training resource etc.

....

How did you hear about Super Series 3?:

Word of mouth: ☐   Through my tutor/trainer: ☐   Mailshot: ☐

Other (please give details): ....

....

Many thanks for your help in returning this form.